═══MADE EASY PRESS═══

2024 • 2025

Monthly Planner

On this day in history

Two-Year Schedule Organizer with Holidays and Daily Historical Events to Keep Track of Your Appointments, Goals, and Activities

 Producer & International Distributor
eBookPro Publishing
www.ebook-pro.com

2024-2025 Monthly Planner — On This Day in History:
Two-Year Schedule Organizer with Holidays and Daily Historical Events to Keep Track of Your Appointments, Goals, and Activities

Made Easy Press

Copyright © 2023 Made Easy Press

All rights reserved; No parts of this book may be reproduced or transmitted in any form or by any means, electronic or mechanical, including photocopying, recording, taping, or by any information retrieval system, without the permission, in writing, of the author.

Contact: agency@ebook-pro.com
ISBN 9789655753943

2024

January

su	mo	tu	we	th	fr	sa
	1	2	3	4	5	6
7	8	9	10	11	12	13
14	15	16	17	18	19	20
21	22	23	24	25	26	27
28	29	30	31			

February

su	mo	tu	we	th	fr	sa
				1	2	3
4	5	6	7	8	9	10
11	12	13	14	15	16	17
18	19	20	21	22	23	24
25	26	27	28	29		

March

su	mo	tu	we	th	fr	sa
					1	2
3	4	5	6	7	8	9
10	11	12	13	14	15	16
17	18	19	20	21	22	23
24	25	26	27	28	29	30
31						

April

su	mo	tu	we	th	fr	sa
	1	2	3	4	5	6
7	8	9	10	11	12	13
14	15	16	17	18	19	20
21	22	23	24	25	26	27
28	29	30				

May

su	mo	tu	we	th	fr	sa
			1	2	3	4
5	6	7	8	9	10	11
12	13	14	15	16	17	18
19	20	21	22	23	24	25
26	27	28	29	30	31	

June

su	mo	tu	we	th	fr	sa
						1
2	3	4	5	6	7	8
9	10	11	12	13	14	15
16	17	18	19	20	21	22
23	24	25	26	27	28	29
30						

July

su	mo	tu	we	th	fr	sa
	1	2	3	4	5	6
7	8	9	10	11	12	13
14	15	16	17	18	19	20
21	22	23	24	25	26	27
28	29	30	31			

August

su	mo	tu	we	th	fr	sa
				1	2	3
4	5	6	7	8	9	10
11	12	13	14	15	16	17
18	19	20	21	22	23	24
25	26	27	28	29	30	31

September

su	mo	tu	we	th	fr	sa
1	2	3	4	5	6	7
8	9	10	11	12	13	14
15	16	17	18	19	20	21
22	23	24	25	26	27	28
29	30					

October

su	mo	tu	we	th	fr	sa
		1	2	3	4	5
6	7	8	9	10	11	12
13	14	15	16	17	18	19
20	21	22	23	24	25	26
27	28	29	30	31		

November

su	mo	tu	we	th	fr	sa
					1	2
3	4	5	6	7	8	9
10	11	12	13	14	15	16
17	18	19	20	21	22	23
24	25	26	27	28	29	30

December

su	mo	tu	we	th	fr	sa
1	2	3	4	5	6	7
8	9	10	11	12	13	14
15	16	17	18	19	20	21
22	23	24	25	26	27	28
29	30	31				

2025

January

su	mo	tu	we	th	fr	sa
			1	2	3	4
5	6	7	8	9	10	11
12	13	14	15	16	17	18
19	20	21	22	23	24	25
26	27	28	29	30	31	

February

su	mo	tu	we	th	fr	sa
						1
2	3	4	5	6	7	8
9	10	11	12	13	14	15
16	17	18	19	20	21	22
23	24	25	26	27	28	

March

su	mo	tu	we	th	fr	sa
						1
2	3	4	5	6	7	8
9	10	11	12	13	14	15
16	17	18	19	20	21	22
23	24	25	26	27	28	29
30	31					

April

su	mo	tu	we	th	fr	sa
		1	2	3	4	5
6	7	8	9	10	11	12
13	14	15	16	17	18	19
20	21	22	23	24	25	26
27	28	29	30			

May

su	mo	tu	we	th	fr	sa
				1	2	3
4	5	6	7	8	9	10
11	12	13	14	15	16	17
18	19	20	21	22	23	24
25	26	27	28	29	30	31

June

su	mo	tu	we	th	fr	sa
1	2	3	4	5	6	7
8	9	10	11	12	13	14
15	16	17	18	19	20	21
22	23	24	25	26	27	28
29	30					

July

su	mo	tu	we	th	fr	sa
		1	2	3	4	5
6	7	8	9	10	11	12
13	14	15	16	17	18	19
20	21	22	23	24	25	26
27	28	29	30	31		

August

su	mo	tu	we	th	fr	sa
					1	2
3	4	5	6	7	8	9
10	11	12	13	14	15	16
17	18	19	20	21	22	23
24	25	26	27	28	29	30
31						

September

su	mo	tu	we	th	fr	sa
	1	2	3	4	5	6
7	8	9	10	11	12	13
14	15	16	17	18	19	20
21	22	23	24	25	26	27
28	29	30				

October

su	mo	tu	we	th	fr	sa
			1	2	3	4
5	6	7	8	9	10	11
12	13	14	15	16	17	18
19	20	21	22	23	24	25
26	27	28	29	30	31	

November

su	mo	tu	we	th	fr	sa
						1
2	3	4	5	6	7	8
9	10	11	12	13	14	15
16	17	18	19	20	21	22
23	24	25	26	27	28	29
30						

December

su	mo	tu	we	th	fr	sa
	1	2	3	4	5	6
7	8	9	10	11	12	13
14	15	16	17	18	19	20
21	22	23	24	25	26	27
28	29	30	31			

Birthday Log

January

February

March

April

May

June

Birthday Log

July

August

September

October

November

December

My 2024 Resolutions

1. ....
2. ....
3. ....
4. ....
5. ....
6. ....
7. ....
8. ....
9. ....
10. ....
11. ....
12. ....
13. ....
14. ....
15. ....
16. ....
17. ....
18. ....

> "You are never too old to set another goal or to dream a new dream."
>
> — C. S. Lewis

January

monday	tuesday	wednesday	thursday
1 New Year's Day	2	3	4
8	9	10	11
15 Martin Luther King Day	16	17	18
22	23	24	25
29	30	31	

2024

friday	saturday	sunday
5	6	7
12	13	14
19	20	21
26	27	28

January

This Month in History

1	45 BC	The Julian calendar took effect for the first time.
2	1959	The Soviet spacecraft Luna 1 was the first to reach the vicinity of the moon.
3	1996	The first mobile flip phone, the Motorola StarTAC, went on sale.
4	2004	NASA's Mars rover, Spirit, made a successful landing on Mars.
5	1757	King Louis XV of France survived a failed assassination attempt.
6	1941	US President Franklin Roosevelt made his famous "Four Freedoms" speech.
7	1610	Galileo Galilei discovered the four Galilean moons of Jupiter: Io, Europa, Ganymede, and Callisto.
8	1942	Renowned physicist Stephen Hawking was born.
9	2005	The Second Sudanese War ended and Southern Sudan was granted autonomy.
10	1863	The first underground railway, the London Underground, opened.
11	1935	Amelia Earhart became the first person to fly solo from Hawaii to the U.S. mainland.
12	1896	The first X-ray photo was taken in the U.S. by Dr. Henry Smith.
13	2000	Bill Gates stepped down as CEO of Microsoft.
14	1559	Elizabeth I was crowned the Queen of England.
15	1892	The rules of basketball were officially published in Springfield, Massachusetts.

16	27	*The Roman Empire was established.*
17	1912	*Captain Robert Scott's expedition arrives at the South Pole, never to leave.*
18	1960	*The U.S. and Japan signed a joint defense treaty.*
19	1937	*Howard Hughes flew from Los Angeles to New York in seven hours and 22 minutes.*
20	1942	*Nazi officials met in the Wannsee, Berlin to discuss the "Final Solution."*
21	1677	*The first American medical journal was published in the form of a pamphlet on smallpox in Boston.*
22	1901	*Queen Victoria of England passed away.*
23	1969	*NASA unveiled its moon-landing craft.*
24	1965	*Winston Churchill died from a cerebral thrombosis at the age of 90.*
25	1947	*The first arcade game, "Cathode ray tube amusement device", was patented by Thomas Goldsmith.*
26	1905	*The world's largest diamond, valued at $2 billion, was mined in South Africa.*
27	1945	*Soviet forces liberated the Auschwitz Nazi death camp.*
28	1921	*Albert Einstein suggests the possibility of measuring the universe for the first time.*
29	1950	*Riots broke out in Johannesburg, South Africa, against the policy of Apartheid.*
30	1933	*Adolf Hitler was named German Chancellor.*
31	1961	*Ham the chimpanzee was sent into outer space on a test flight and returned safely.*

February — Black History Month

monday	tuesday	wednesday	thursday
			1
5	6	7	8
12	13 Mardi Gras	14 Valentine's Day	15
19 Presidents Day	20	21	22
26	27	28	29

2024

friday	saturday	sunday
2 Groundhog Day	3	4
9	10	11
16	17	18
23	24	25

February

This Month in History

1	1979	Ayatollah Khomeini returned to Iran after 15 years in exilem, marking the beginning of the Iranian Revolution.
2	1852	The first public flushing toilet opened in London.
3	1690	The first paper money in America was issued in the Massachusetts Bay Colony.
4	2004	The social network Facebook was founded.
5	1971	Two Apollo 14 astronauts walk on the moon, two years after the first moonwalk.
6	1899	The Spanish-American War ended.
7	1963	The Mona Lisa was displayed at the New York Metropolitan Museum of Art.
8	1910	The Boy Scouts of America was founded, 3 years after it was founded in England.
9	1969	The Boeing 747, the "Jumbo Jet," flew for the first time.
10	1996	"Deep Blue" was the first computer to win a chess game against a reigning world champion.
11	1990	Nelson Mandela was freed after 27 years in prison as a political prisoner.
12	1994	Edvard Munch's iconic painting "The Scream" was stolen and recovered several months later.
13	1542	Catherine Howard, Henry VIII's fifth wife, was beheaded for adultery.
14	1979	Armed forces launched an attack on the U.S. embassy in Tehran.

15	2003	30 million people in 600 countries protested against the Iraq War.
16	1985	The Lebanese political party and militant group Hezbollah was founded.
17	1992	Serial killer Jeffrey Dahmer was sent to jail for life.
18	1885	"The Adventures of Huckleberry Finn" by Mark Twain was published in New York.
19	1903	The Austria-Hungary government declared a mandatory two-year military service.
20	1792	The U.S. Postal Service was formed.
21	1965	Civil rights leader Malcolm X was assassinated during a speech in Manhattan.
22	1935	President Roosevelt barred all flights over the White House as they disturbed his sleep.
23	1955	Eight nations met in Bangkok for the first SEATO (Southeast Asia Treaty Organization) council.
24	1895	The Cuban War of Independence began.
25	1791	President George Washington signed a bill creating the Bank of the United States.
26	1972	The Luna 20 Soviet spacecraft returned successfully to Earth bearing rock samples from the moon.
27	1908	The forty-sixth star, representing the state of Oklahoma, was added to the U.S. flag.
28	1066	Westminster Abbey in London opened its doors.
29	1968	The Beatles won a Grammy Award for their album "Sergeant Pepper's Lonely Hearts Club Band".

March

Women's History Month

monday	tuesday	wednesday	thursday
4	5	6	7
11	12	13	14
Ramadan			
18	19	20	21
25	26	27	28

Irish American Heritage Month　　　2024

friday	saturday	sunday
1	2	3
8	9	10 Daylight Saving Starts
15	16	17 St. Patrick's Day
22	23	24 Purim
29 Good Friday	30	31 Easter

March

This Month in History

1	1893	Iventor Nikola Tesla first publicly demonstrated radio during a meeting of the National Electric Light Association in St. Louis.
2	1962	Rock singer Jon Bon Jovi was born.
3	1931	"The Star-Spangled Banner" officially became the national anthem of the United States.
4	1865	President Abraham Lincoln was inaugurated for a second term in office.
5	1971	NASA's Voyager 1 space probe flew past Jupiter and transmitted photographs of the planet and its moons.
6	1912	Oreo sandwich cookies were first introduced by the National Biscuit Co.
7	1876	Alexander Graham Bell received a U.S. patent for his invention of the telephone.
8	1965	The first U.S. combat troops landed in South Vietnam.
9	1562	Kissing in public was officially banned in Naples, Italy, with the transgression punishable by death.
10	1969	James Earl Ray pleaded guilty to assassinating civil rights leader Martin Luther King Jr.
11	1997	Rock star Paul McCartney was knighted by Queen Elizabeth II.
12	1912	The first American Girl Scouts troop was formed.
13	1639	Cambridge College in Massachusetts was renamed "Harvard" after clergyman John Harvard.
14	1794	Eli Whitney patented the cotton gin, which would revolutionize modern industry.
15	44 B.C	Julius Caeser was assassinated in Rome by a group of nobles.

16	1984	*William Buckley, the CIA station chief in Beirut, was kidnapped by Hezbollah militants.*
17	1969	*Golda Meir became the first female prime minister of Israel.*
18	1940	*Adolf Hitler and Benito Mussolini agreed to join forces in the war against France and Britain.*
19	2003	*President George W. Bush ordered the start of the war against Iraq.*
20	1969	*Beatles singer John Lennon married Yoko Ono in Gibraltar.*
21	1685	*Composer Johann Sebastian Bach was born in Eisenach, Germany.*
22	1963	*The Beatles' debut album, "Please Please Me," was released in the United Kingdom by Parlophone.*
23	1998	*"Titanic" won eleven Academy Awards, including best picture and best song.*
24	1934	*President Franklin D. Roosevelt signed a bill granting future independence to the Philippines.*
25	1954	*Production of the first color televisions began in Indiana.*
26	1827	*Composer Johann Sebastian Bach was born in Eisenach, Germany.*
27	1964	*Alaska was hit by the strongest-ever recorded earthquake, at magnitude 9.2, causing multiple tsunamis.*
28	1987	*Maria Von Trapp, whose life inspired the movie "The Sound of Music," died at age 82.*
29	1867	*Queen Victoria of England signed the British North America Act, creating the Dominion of Canada.*
30	1981	*President Ronald Reagan was shot and injured by John W. Hinckley Jr. outside a Washington, D.C. hotel.*
31	2020	*Britain's Prince Harry and his wife Meghan officially stepped down from duties as members of the royal family.*

April

monday	tuesday	wednesday	thursday
1 April Fool's Day	2	3	4
8	9	10 Eid al-Fitr	11
15	16	17	18
22 Earth Day	23 Passover	24	25
29	30		

2024

friday	saturday	sunday
5	6	7
12	13	14
19	20	21
26	27	28

April

This Month in History

1	2001	The Netherlands became the first country in the world to allow same-sex marriage.
2	1792	The U.S. dollar is introduced under the Mint Act.
3	1922	Joseph Stalin was appointed General Secretary of the Russian Communist Party by Vladimir Lenin.
4	1968	Martin Luther King Jr. was assassinated by James Earl Ray.
5	1722	Dutch explorer Jacob Roggeveen discovered the mysterious Easter Islands in the southeastern Pacific.
6	1896	The first modern Olympic Games opened in Athens, 15 centuries after the last ancient Olmpic Games were held.
7	30	Jesus is estimated to have been crucified in Jerusalem on this date.
8	1879	Milk was sold in glass bottles for the first time.
9	1860	The earliest sound recording device, the phonautograph, captured the first recording of a human voice.
10	2001	Euthanasia became legal in the Netherlands.
11	1912	The RMS Titanic set off on its first and only journey from Ireland to New York.
12	1961	Yuri Gagarin boarded the Vostok-3KA spacecraft to become the first human in space.
13	1997	Tiger Woods won the Masters Golf Tournament, becoming the youngest player to do so at age 21.
14	1986	Bangladesh was hit by the heaviest hail ever recorded, weighing over 2lb each.

15	1947	Jackie Robinson became the first African-American to play in a US major league baseball game.
16	1900	The U.S. Post Office issued the first postage stamps.
17	1986	The world's longest war, between the Netherlands and the Isles of Scilly, ended after 335 years.
18	1956	Grace Kelly and Rainier III, the Prince of Monaco, got married.
19	1775	The American Revolutionary War began with the battles of Lexington and Concord.
20	1999	The Columbine High Massacre is carried out in Colorado.
21	1934	The famous alleged picture of the Loch Ness Monster was published in the Daily Mail.
22	1997	The Japanese embassy hostage crisis ended after 126 tense days.
23	2005	The first YouTube video was posted from the San Diego Zoo.
24	2018	Music streaming services overtook worldwide sales of CDs and vinyl.
25	1792	The guillotine was used for the first time in France.
26	1986	Reactor 4 at the Chernobyl nuclear power plant exploded, causing the worst nuclear disaster in history.
27	1810	Ludwig van Beethoven finished composing his masterpiece, "Für Elise".
28	1848	Slavery was abolished in all French territories.
29	1968	The musical "Hair" performed on Broadway for the first time.
30	1859	"A Tale of Two Cities" by Charles Dickens was published in a literary periodical.

May

Military Appreciation Month

monday	tuesday	wednesday	thursday
		1	2
6	7	8	9
13	14	15	16
20	21	22	23
27 Memorial Day	28	29	30

2024

friday	saturday	sunday
3	4	5 Cinco de Mayo
10	11	12 Mother's Day
17	18 Armed Forces Day	19 Pentecost
24	25	26
31		

May

This Month in History

1	1840	The world's first adhesive postage stamp was issued in the UK.
2	2011	U.S. commando forces killed Al-Qaeda founder, Osama Bin Laden, in Pakistan.
3	1898	Golda Meir, the future prime minister of Israel, was born.
4	1715	A French manufacturer patented the first folding umbrella.
5	1821	Napoleon Bonaparte died while still in exile on the island of St. Helena.
6	2004	The final episode of the hit sitcom "Friends" aired and was watched by 52 million viewers.
7	1429	Joan of Arc and the French army broke the English siege of Orleans.
8	1978	Reinhold Messner and Peter Habeler became the first people to climb Mount Everest without any oxygen supply.
9	1960	The first birth control pill, "Enovid," was approved by the FDA.
10	1869	The first coast to coast railroad in the U.S. is completed.
11	1960	Nazi mastermind Adolf Eichmann was captured in Argentina by Israeli Mossad and military.
12	1935	"Alcoholics Anonymous" was founded in Ohio by a stockbroker and a heart surgeon.
13	1888	Slavery was abolished in Brazil.
14	1796	The first smallpox vaccine was administered to an 8-year-old boy.
15	1958	The Sputnik III satellite was launched into space by the Soviet Union.

16	1929	The first Academy Awards were held in Hollywood, with winners including Charlie Chaplin and the Warner Brothers.
17	1792	The New York Stock Exchange was formed by merchants on Wall Street.
18	1974	India became the sixth nation to successfully detonate an atomic bomb.
19	1780	New England mysteriously descended into complete darkness in a still unexplained event.
20	1940	The first prisoners arrived at Auschwitz concentration camp in Poland.
21	1932	Amelia Earhart became the first woman to fly solo nonstop across the Atlantic
22	1980	Pac-Man is released as an arcade game.
23	1945	Heinrich Himmler, the head of the Nazi Gestapo, commited suicide upon capture by Allied forces.
24	1830	Sarah Josepha Hale published the nursery rhyme "Mary Had a Little Lamb."
25	1977	George Lucas' first Star Wars film, later titled "A New Hope", premiered.
26	1908	The first major Middle East oil reserve was discovered by engineers in Iran.
27	1937	The Golden Gate Bridge in San Francisco was opened.
28	1805	Napoleon Bonaparte was crowned in Milan, Italy.
29	1953	Edmund Hillary successfully ascended to Mount Everest's summit, becoming the first person to do so.
30	1431	Patron Saint of France, Joan of Arc, was killed by the English.
31	1879	Madison Square Garden in New York opened its doors.

June   *Pride Month*

monday	tuesday	wednesday	thursday
3	4	5	6
10	11	12 Shavuot	13
17 Eid al-Adha	18	19	20
24	25	26	27

2024

friday	saturday	sunday
	1	2
7	8	9
14	15	16
Flag Day		Father's Day
21	22	23
28	29	30

June

This Month in History

1	1974	The anti-choking Heimlich maneuver was presented to the public.
2	1847	Mendelssohn's "Wedding March" was played for the first time at a wedding ceremony.
3	1982	The Israeli ambassador to the U.K. was shot, triggering the First Lebanon War.
4	1989	Poland held its first free elections since World War II.
5	1968	Robert F. Kennedy, the brother of former U.S. President John F. Kennedy, was assassinated.
6	1946	The National Basketball Association (NBA) was founded.
7	1929	Vatican City signed the Lateran Treaty to become an independent state.
8	1972	Nick Út captured the famous "napalm girl" photograph in Vietnam.
9	1934	Donald Duck appeared for the first time in film.
10	1909	An SOS signal was transmitted for the first time in an emergency.
11	1963	Martin Luther King was arrested in Florida for his attempt to integrate restaurants.
12	1849	The gas mask was patented by Lewis P. Haslett.
13	1983	The Pioneer 10, which had already been in space for 11 years, left the Solar System.
14	1949	The State of Vietnam was formed.
15	1836	Arkansas was admitted into the Union as the 25th state.

16	1952	*Anne Frank's diary was published in the U.S.*
17	1950	*The first kidney transplant was carried out by a surgeon in Chicago.*
18	1815	*The Battle of Waterloo ended in a disastrous defeat for Napoleon.*
19	1846	*The first baseball game is played in Hoboken, New Jersey.*
20	1975	*Steven Spielberg's classic film, "Jaws," premiered.*
21	1982	*Prince William, the Duke of Cambridge and future King of England, was born.*
22	1981	*Mark David Chapman pleaded guilty to killing John Lennon.*
23	2016	*The UK made the historic Brexit vote, opting to leave the European Union.*
24	1987	*Argentina's star soccer player Lionel Messi was born.*
25	1993	*Turkey and Canada both elected their first female heads of government.*
26	1906	*The first Grand Prix car race was held in Le Mans, Paris.*
27	1954	*The world's first nuclear power plant in Russia was activated*
28	1846	*The saxophone was patented by Belgian musician Adolphe Sax.*
29	2007	*Steve Jobs and Apple released the first iPhone.*
30	1908	*The mysterious Tunguska event, believed to have been caused by an asteroid or comet collision, left 500 acres of land in Siberia flattened.*

July

monday	tuesday	wednesday	thursday
1	2	3	4 Independence Day
8 Muharram	9	10	11
15	16	17	18
22	23	24	25
29	30	31	

2024

friday	saturday	sunday
5	6	7
12	13	14 Bastille Day
19	20	21
26	27	28 Parents' Day

July

This Month in History

1	1966	The Medicare federal insurance program went into effect.
2	1881	President James A. Garfield was shot and killed by Charles J. Guiteau at a train station.
3	1986	A gala ceremony was held in New York Harbor to celebrate the relighting of the renovated Statue of Liberty.
4	1802	The United States Military Academy officially opened at West Point, New York.
5	2008	Tennis-playing sisters Venus and Serena Williams competed for the Wimbledon singles final, with Venus taking the win.
6	1483	King Richard III was crowned in Westminster Abbey in England.
7	1976	The West Point Military Academy accepted 119 female cadets for the first time.
8	1776	Colonel John Nixon gave the first public reading of the Declaration of Independence outside Independence Hall.
9	1947	Princess Elizabeth of Britain announced her engagement to Lt. Philip Mountbatten.
10	2018	Twelve boys and their soccer coach were rescued from a cave in Thailand after being trapped for over two weeks.
11	1804	Alexander Hamilton was fatally wounded in a duel by Vice President Aaron Burr.
12	1862	President Abraham Lincoln signed a bill authorizing the Army Medal of Honor.
13	1985	The international "Live Aid" rock concert took place in several locations around the world to raise money to combat starvation in Africa.
14	2020	Moderna's COVID-19 vaccine was declared to be effective.
15	1997	Fashion designer Gianni Versace was shot and killed outside his home in Miami.

16	1969	*Apollo 11 set off for its moon mission from Cape Kennedy.*
17	1955	*Disneyland park was opened for the first time in Anaheim, California.*
18	1925	*Adolf Hitler published his autobiography, "Mein Kampf."*
19	1980	*Dozens of nations boycotted the Moscow Summer Olympics due to the Soviet military intervention in Afghanistan.*
20	1969	*Astronauts Neil Armstrong and Edwin "Buzz" Aldrin became the first men to walk on the moon.*
21	2002	*The British Open Tennis tournament ended in sudden-death for the first time in the tournament's 142 years.*
22	1992	*Prince George was born to William and Kate, the duke and duchess of Cambridge, taking his place as third in line to the British throne.*
23	1999	*Astronaut Eileen Collins became the first woman to command a U.S. space flight.*
24	1866	*Tennessee became the first state to be readmitted to the Union after the Civil War.*
25	1946	*The U.S. conducted the first underwater atomic bomb in the Pacific Ocean.*
26	1990	*President George H.W. Bush signed the Americans with Disabilities Act.*
27	2012	*The opening ceremony of the Summer Olympics in London opened with stunt doubles dressed as James Bond and Queen Elizabeth parachuting down from the sky.*
28	1914	*World War I began when Austria-Hungary declared war on Serbia.*
29	1958	*President Eisenhower signed the National Aeronautics and Space Act, officially forming NASA.*
30	1980	*Israel's Parliament passed a law reaffirming the entire city of Jerusalem as the capital of the Jewish state.*
31	1981	*A seven-week Major League Baseball strike ended.*

August

monday	tuesday	wednesday	thursday
			1
5	6	7	8
12	13	14	15
19	20	21	22
26	27	28	29

2024

friday	saturday	sunday
2	3	4
9	10	11
16	17	18
23	24	25
30	31	

August

This Month in History

1	1936	Adolf Hitler attended the opening ceremony of the Summer Olympics of 1936.
2	1990	Iraq invaded and seized control of Quwait.
3	1492	Christopher Columbus set sail from Spain on a voyage that would lead him to discover America.
4	1944	15-year-old Anne Frank and her family were found and arrested by the Gestapo in Amsterdam.
5	1962	South African activist Nelson Mandela was arrested for leaving the country without a passport and would later be imprisoned for 27 years.
6	1825	Upper Peru became the autonomous republic of Bolivia.
7	2012	Aly Raisman became the first U.S. woman gymnast to win Olympic gold on floor.
8	1963	Britain's "Great Train Robbery" took place as thieves made off with 2.6 million pounds in banknotes.
9	1945	The second nuclear bomb was dropped on Nagasaki, killing 74,000 people.
10	1993	Ruth Bader Ginsburg was sworn in as the second female justice on the U.S. Supreme Court.
11	1934	Alcatraz Prison welcomed its first federal prisoners after changing its status from a military prison.
12	1985	The world's deadliest single-aircraft disaster killed 520 passengers of a Japan Airlines Boeing 747.
13	1846	The American flag was raised in Los Angeles for the first time.
14	1947	Pakistan gained its independence from Britain.
15	1969	The first Woodstock Music and Art Fair opened in upstate New York.

16	1977	Elvis Presley died in his Graceland estate in Tennessee, aged 42.
17	1999	More than 17,000 people were killed when a magnitude 7.4 earthquake struck Turkey.
18	1920	The 19th Amendment to the U.S. Constitution was ratified, granting women the right to vote.
19	2010	The last American combat brigade left Iraq for good.
20	1866	The Civil War was declared over by President Andrew Johnson.
21	1911	The Mona Lisa was stolen from the Louvre in Paris, to be reovered only two years later.
22	1787	The first steamboat was presented by inventor John Fitch on the Delaware River.
23	1914	Japan declared war against Germany in World War I.
24	24 A.D.	Mount Vesuvius erupted, burying the entire city of Pompeii.
25	1928	Richard E. Byrde's expedition to Antarctican set sail from the shore of New Jersey.
26	1944	The French general Charles de Gaulle led a victory march in Paris after its liberation from Nazi occupation.
27	1967	The Beatles' manager, Brian Epstein, was found dead in his apartment from an accidental overdose.
28	2016	Six scientists completed a yearlong experiment living in an isolated dome to simulate life on Mars.
29	1958	Future pop star Michael Jackson was born in Indiana.
30	1983	Guion Bluford Jr. embarked Challenger to become the first Black American astronaut in space.
31	2010	President Barack Obama ended the U.S. combat mission in Iraq.

September

monday	tuesday	wednesday	thursday
2	3	4	5
Labor Day			
9	10	11	12
		Patriot Day	
16	17	18	19
Stepfamily Day	Citizenship Day		
23	24	25	26
30			

2024

friday	saturday	sunday
		1
6	7	8 Grandparents' Day
13	14	15
20	21	22
27	28	29

September

This Month in History

1	1939	Nazi Germany invaded Poland and World War II began.
2	1789	The United States Treasury Department was established.
3	1783	The United States and Britain signed the Treaty of Paris, ending the Revolutionary War.
4	2006	Australian "Crocodile Hunter" Steve Irwin died following an encounter with a stingray.
5	1972	The terrorist group Black September attacked and killed 11 members of the Israel Olympic delegation in Munich.
6	1991	The Soviet Uniongranted independence to Lithuania, Latvia and Estonia.
7	1940	The German air blitz on London in World War II began.
8	1504	Michelangelo's famous statue of David was unveiled in Florence, Italy.
9	1850	California became the 31st American state.
10	1846	The sewing machine was patented by Elias Howe.
11	2001	The World Trade Center was attacked by terrorist group al-Qaida.
12	2013	The Voyager 1 became the first man-made object outside the solar system.
13	1996	Rapper Tupac Shakur died in hospital after suffering a fatal gunshot wound at age 25.
14	1939	The first prefrontal lobotomy in the U.S. was performed at George Washington University Hospital.
15	1835	Charles Darwin reached the Galapagos Islands aboard the HMS Beagle.

16	1997	*Steve Jobs was named Apple Computer Inc.'s CEO.*
17	1939	*Taisto Mäki broke a record by running 10k in under 30 minutes.*
18	1812	*The Great Fire of Moscow finally burnt out after 5 days, with 75% of the city destroyed.*
19	1893	*New Zealand became the first country to grant women the right to vote.*
20	1990	*The reunification of East and West Germany went into effect.*
21	1915	*The historical Stonehenge monument was bought by Cecil Chubb for £6,600.*
22	1965	*The Indo-Pakistani war officially came to a close.*
23	1889	*The Nintendo company was founded by Fusajiro Yamauchi.*
24	1789	*The US Attorney General Office was formed.*
25	1992	*NASA launched the Mars Observer probe, which failed 11 months later.*
26	1949	*The old "Hollywoodland" sign was torn down and replaced with just "Hollywood."*
27	1066	*William the Conqueror's troops set sail from Normandy on a quest to conquer England.*
28	1968	*The Beatles song, "Hey Jude," hit number one and would stay there for nine weeks.*
29	1994	*MS Estonia, a passenger and car ferry, sank in the Baltic Sea in the worst maritime disaster of the 20th century.*
30	1846	*Anesthetic was used for the first time by a dentist removing a tooth.*

October

monday	tuesday	wednesday	thursday
	1	2	3 Rosh Hashana
7	8	9	10
14 Columbus Day	15	16	17 Sukkot
21	22	23	24
28	29	30	31 Halloween

2024

friday	saturday	sunday
4	5	6
11	12 Yom Kippur	13
18	19	20
25	26	27

October

This Month in History

1	1949	Mao Zedong declared the establishment of the People's Republic of China.
2	1950	The first "Peanuts" comic strip was published, featuring Charlie Brown, with Snoopy appearing two days later.
3	1863	President Lincoln proclaimed the last Thursday of November as Thanksgiving Day.
4	1895	The first US Open Golf tournament was held in Newport, Rhode Island.
5	1969	The British comedy series, Monty Python's Flying Circus, premiered on BBC.
6	1973	Egypt, Syria, Iraq, and Jordan launched a surprise attack on Israel, opening the Yom Kippur War.
7	1996	Fox News broadcasted for the very first time.
8	1948	The world's first internal pacemaker was implanted in Sweden.
9	2012	Malala Yousafzai survived an assassination attempt and went on to win a Nobel Prize.
10	1845	The U.S. Naval Academy was founded.
11	1975	The first episode of Saturday Night Live aired, with the cast including Dan Aykroyd, John Belushi, and Chevy Chase.
12	1609	Believed to be the first non-religious song ever printed, "Three Blind Mice" was published in London.
13	1958	Paddington Bear first appeared in literature.
14	1966	Canada opened its underground Montreal Metro rapid-transit system.
15	1844	Friedrich Nietzsche was born in the small German village of Röcken bei Lützen.

16	1986	Reinhold Messner became the first person to scale all 14 highest mountains in the world.
17	1933	Albert Einstein immigrated to the U.S. from Germany, settling in New Jersey.
18	1967	A Russian spacecraft made the first-ever landing on the surface of Venus.
19	1917	The first doughnut was fried by Salvation Army volunteers in France during World War I.
20	1973	The Sydney Opera House opened its doors.
21	1967	50,000 demonstrators converged outside the Pentagon in protest over American involvement in Vietnam.
22	1938	Chester Carlson invented the photocopier.
23	1783	Virginia emancipated its slaves who fought for independence in the Revolutionary War.
24	1945	The United Nations was founded with 5 permanent members and 46 member states.
25	1954	President Eisenhower led the first televised Cabinet meeting.
26	1984	Baby Fae received a heart from a babboon, becoming the first infant to receive an organ from another species.
27	1904	The New York City subway system began operating.
28	2007	Argentina elected its first female president, the former first lady Cristina Fernández de Kirchner.
29	1998	John Glenn flew aboard the Discovery shuttle at the age of 77 years, making him the oldest person in space.
30	1270	The Seventh Crusade was ended by the Treaty of Barbary.
31	2011	The world's population officially reached 7 billion people.

November

monday	tuesday	wednesday	thursday
4	5	6	7
11 Veterans' Day	12	13	14
18	19	20	21
25	26	27	28 Thanksgiving

2024

friday	saturday	sunday
1	2	3 Daylight Saving Ends
8	9	10
15	16	17
22	23	24
29 Black Friday	30	

November

This Month in History

1	1894	Nicholas II became the Tsar of Russia.
2	1984	Serial killer Velma Barfield became one of the only women executed in the U.S.
3	1973	NASA launched Mariner 10, the first probe to reach planet Mercury.
4	2008	Barack Obama became the first Black president of the United States.
5	1930	Sinclair Lewis was the first American to win a Nobel Prize in Literature for his novel Babbit.
6	1860	Abraham Lincoln was elected 16th president of the United States.
7	1940	The Tacoma Bridge in Washington collapsed.
8	1939	Johann Georg Elser, a German woodworker, made a failed assassination attempt on Adolf Hitler's life.
9	1938	The pogrom known as "Kristallnacht", or "Night of Broken Glass" was carried out in Germany and Austria.
10	1775	The U.S. Marine Corps was founded in Philadelphia during the American Revolutionary War.
11	1918	World War I officially ended.
12	1927	Canada was officially admitted to the League of Nations.
13	1907	The first helicopter flight is achieved by Paul Corno.
14	1969	NASA launched Apollo 12, the second moon mission.
15	1988	The Palestinian Liberation Organization (PLO) declared the creation of the state of Palestine.

#	Year	Event
16	2001	The first Harry Potter film, "Harry Potter and the Philosopher's Stone", was released.
17	1869	The Suez Canal was formally opened.
18	1928	Mickey Mouse made his film debut in "Steamboat Willie", the first animated talking picture.
19	1969	Brazilian soccer player Pelé made his 1,000th professional goal.
20	1923	The automated traffic signal, the precursor to the traffic light, was patented.
21	1904	Motorized automobiles replaced horse-drawn cars in Paris.
22	1995	Pixar released the hit film "Toy Story 1".
23	1963	The Doctor Who TV series had its debut, and would become the longest-running science fiction show.
24	1946	Serial killer Ted Bundy was born.
25	1930	690 earthquakes were recorded in one day in Ito, Japan.
26	2003	After 27 years of flight, the Concorde plane was retired from service.
27	2001	Hubble telescope detected sodium on an exoplanet, making it the first recognized planetary atmosphere outside the Solar System.
28	1948	The first Polaroid cameras were available for sale in Boston.
29	1929	Explorer Richard Byrd became the first person to fly over the South Pole.
30	1940	Lucille Ball and Desi Arnaz, the stars of "I Love Lucy," got married.

December

monday	tuesday	wednesday	thursday
2 Cyber Monday	3	4	5
9	10	11	12
16	17	18	19
23	24 Christmas Eve	25	26
30	31 New Year's Eve	Christmas Day	Hanukkah

2024

friday	saturday	sunday
		1
6	7 Pearl Harbor Remembrance Day	8
13	14	15
20	21	22
27	28	29

December

This Month in History

1	1981	The AIDS virus gained official recognition.
2	1939	LaGuardia Airport in New York City opened its doors.
3	1992	A test engineer for Sema Group sent the world's first text message.
4	1791	The first Sunday paper, "The Observer," was published.
5	1933	Prohibition in the U.S. ended with the lifting of the national ban on alcohol.
6	1865	The Thirteenth Amendment, abolishing slavery, was adopted.
7	1941	The Japanese Navy launched an attack on the U.S. naval base in Pearl Harbor.
8	1941	The U.S. declared war on Japan and officially joined World War II.
9	1979	The World Health Organization declared that the smallpox disease had been successfully eradicated.
10	2001	"The Fellowship of the Ring," the first movie in the Lord of the Rings trilogy, premiered.
11	1936	King Edward VIII caused a scandal in England when he abdicated from the throne to marry Wallis Simpson.
12	1915	Frank Sinatra was born.
13	1795	A meteorite crashed into Yorkshire in England.
14	1911	Roald Amundsen and his team became the first people to land on the South Pole.
15	2001	The Leaning Tower of Pisa reopened to visitors after 11 years were spent fortifying it.

16	1773	The Boston Tea Party protest occurred when protestors dumped English tea in the Boston harbor.
17	1903	The Wright brothers flew the first airplane from Kitty Hawk in North Carolina.
18	1946	Renowned film director Steven Spielberg was born.
19	2012	Park Geun-hye was elected as the first female president of South Korea.
20	2007	Queen Elizabeth II became the oldest living British monarch, at 81 years old.
21	1937	Disney released "Snow White and the Seven Dwarves", the first full-length animated film.
22	1891	The first asteroid was discovered with astrophotography by Max Wolf.
23	1922	BBC Radio began daily newscasts.
24	1914	The World War I Christmas Truce between English and German troops began.
25	1643	Christmas Island was discovered Captain William Mynors, named after the date of its discovery.
26	1966	The first Kwanzaa celebrations were held.
27	1978	Spain became a democracy after 40 years of dictatorship.
28	1612	Galileo made the first known observation of Neptune.
29	1845	Texas was admitted to the union as the 28th U.S. state.
30	1984	Basketball legend Lebron James was born.
31	1907	The ball dropped for the first time at Times Square.

My 2025 Resolutions

1 ....
2 ....
3 ....
4 ....
5 ....
6 ....
7 ....
8 ....
9 ....
10 ....
11 ....
12 ....
13 ....
14 ....
15 ....
16 ....
17 ....
18 ....

"Do not wait until the conditions are perfect to begin. Beginnings make the conditions perfect."

— Alan Cohen

January

monday	tuesday	wednesday	thursday
		1 New Year's Day	2
6	7	8	9
13	14	15	16
20 Martin Luther King Day	21	22	23
27	28	29	30

2025

friday	saturday	sunday
3	4	5
10	11	12
17	18	19
24	25	26
31		

January

This Month in History

1	1992	The Russian Federation was formed following the disintegration of the Soviet Union.
2	1981	British police arrested the Yorkshire Ripper serial killer, Peter Sutcliffe.
3	1959	Alaska was admitted into the Union as the 49th and largest state.
4	2010	The Burj Khalifa, the tallest building in the world, opened to the public.
5	1709	Europe's "Great Frost" began during the night, opening the coldest ever recorded winter on the continent.
6	1907	Maria Montessori opened her first school.
7	1979	Vietnamese forces captured the Cambodian capital Phnom Penh.
8	1935	Singer Elvis Presley was born.
9	1861	The first shots of the American Civil War were fired.
10	1929	The first "Adventures of Tintin" comic book by Hergé was published.
11	1922	Insulin was first used to treat diabetes.
12	1908	The first long-distance radio message was broadcast from the Eiffel Tower in Paris.
13	1915	The worst earthquake of the century killed 30,000 people near Rome, Italy.
14	2010	Yemen declared war on al-Qaeda terrorist group.
15	1759	The British Museum opened.

16	1919	The U.S. Constitution's 18th amendment came into effect, starting the prohibition.
17	1945	Soviet and Polish forces liberated Warsaw during World War II.
18	1535	Francisco Pizarro founded the city of Lima in Peru.
19	1923	France announced the invention of a new gun with a firing range of 56 miles.
20	1941	Hitler met with Mussolini to offer aid in Albania and Greece.
21	1789	The first American novel, "The Power of Sympathy" by William Hill Brown, was published by Isaiah Thomas.
22	1973	The U.S. Supreme Court legalized abortion.
23	1859	Mauna Loa volcano in Hawaii began an eruption that would last 300 days.
24	41	Shortly after declaring himself a god, Roman Emperor Caligula was assassinated by two Praetorian tribunes.
25	1924	The first-ever Winter Olympics began in France.
26	1788	The first Europeans settled in Sydney Harbor, Australia.
27	1959	NASA selected 110 candidates for the first U.S. space flight.
28	1912	Abstract expressionist painter Jackson Pollock was born.
29	1929	America's first school for training dogs to guide the blind was founded in Tennessee.
30	1844	Richard Theodore Greener became the first African American to graduate from Harvard University.
31	1865	The 13th amendment to the American Constitution was passed, abolishing slavery.

February

Black History Month

monday	tuesday	wednesday	thursday
3	4	5	6
10	11	12	13
17 Presidents Day	18	19	20
24	25	26	27

2025

friday	saturday	sunday
	1	2 Groundhog Day
7	8	9
14 Valentine's Day	15	16
21	22	23
28		

February

This Month in History

1	1884	The first volume of the Oxford English Dictionary, A–Ant, was published.
2	1977	Colombian singer-songwriter Shakira was born.
3	1863	Samuel Clemens first used the pen name "Mark Twain" when he wrote in a newspaper.
4	1789	George Washington was elected the first President of the United States.
5	1961	The Soviets launched the Sputnik V satellite, which was the heaviest at 7.1 tons.
6	1964	Paris and London made the decision to build a rail tunnel under the English Channel.
7	2005	Ellen MacArthur finished her record-breaking round-the-world solo sailing journey.
8	1960	The first 8 stars were added to the Hollywood Walk of Fame.
9	1964	The Beatles began their first tour in the U.S.
10	2009	The U.S. satellite "Iridium 33" collided in space with the Russian satellite "Kosmos 2251", destroying both.
11	1975	Margaret Thatcher became the first woman to lead the British Conservative Party.
12	1931	Japan made its first television broadcast, a baseball game.
13	1914	The American Society of Composers, Authors and Publishers (ASCAP) was founded.
14	270	St. Valentine was executed after signing a letter to his beloved, "from your Valentine", leading to the establishment of Valentine's Day.

15	2001	The first draft of the complete human genome was published.
16	1959	Fidel Castro rose to power as Cuba's Prime Minister.
17	1963	Basketball player Michael Jordan was born.
18	1861	Victor Emmanuel II became the first King of Italy.
19	1926	Dr. Lane of Princeton estimated the earth's age at one billion years.
20	1962	Astronaut John Glenn became the first American to orbit the Earth.
21	1940	The Germans began construction of the Auschwitz concentration camp.
22	1825	Russia and Britain established the Alaska Canada border.
23	1898	Writer Emile Zola was imprisoned for his letter, "J'accuse," which he accused the French government of anti-semitism.
24	1912	Italy drops bombs on Beirut in the first act of war against the Ottoman Empire.
25	1815	Napoleon left his exile on the island of Elba and returned to France.
26	1968	Thirty-two African nations decided to boycott the Olympics due to South Africa's participation.
27	1827	The first Mardi-Gras celebration was held in New Orleans.
28	1861	The territory of Colorado is established.

March   Women's History Month

monday	tuesday	wednesday	thursday
3	4 Mardi Gras	5	6
10	11	12	13
17 St. Patrick's Day	18	19	20
24 31 Eid al-Fitr	25	26	27

Irish American Heritage Month 2025

friday	saturday	sunday
	1	2
	Ramadan	
7	8	9
		Daylight Saving Starts
14	15	16
Purim		
21	22	23
28	29	30

March

This Month in History

1	2020	New York City had its first confirmed case of the coronavirus.
2	1962	Wilt Chamberlain scored 100 points for the Philadelphia Warriors in a game against the New York Knicks, setting an NBA record that has not yet been broken.
3	2017	The Nintendo Switch made its debut.
4	1933	Franklin D. Roosevelt was sworn in as America's 32nd president.
5	1933	The Nazi Party won the German parliamentary elections.
6	1964	Boxing champion Cassius Clay officially changed his name to Muhammad Ali.
7	1916	Bavarian Motor Works (BMW) was established in Munich, Germany as an airplane engine manufacturer.
8	1817	The New York Stock Exchange was formally organized.
9	1916	Germany declared war against Portugal.
10	1997	"Buffy the Vampire Slayer" premiered on WB Television Network.
11	2011	A huge tsunami hit Japan's northeastern coast, resulting in 20,000 deaths and damage to a nuclear power station.
12	1987	The musical play "Les Miserables" opened on Broadway.
13	1781	The seventh planet of the solar system, Uranus, was discovered by Sir William Herschel.
14	1879	Albert Einstein was born in Germany.
15	1972	"The Godfather" movie starring Marlon Brando and Al Pacino premiered in New York.
16	1521	Portuguese explorer Ferdinand Magellan and his crew reached the Philippines.

17	2016	SeaWorld Entertainment declared that it would stop breeding killer whales and making them perform tricks.
18	1965	Alexei Leonov carried out the first-ever spacewalk, secured to his capsule by a tether.
19	1911	The first "International Women's Day" was celebrated.
20	1413	King Henry IV of England died and was succeeded by Henry V.
21	1935	Persia changed its name officially to Iran.
22	1894	The first hockey Stanley Cup championship game was played.
23	1993	Scientists announced they had found the gene that causes the incurable Huntington's disease.
24	2020	The International Olympic Committee announced that the Tokyo Summer Olympics would be postponed until 2021 due to the coronavirus.
25	1655	Astronomer Christiaan Huygens discovered Titan, Saturn's biggest moon.
26	1979	A peace treaty was signed between Israel and Egypt at the White House, overseen by President Jimmy Carter.
27	1973	Marlon Brando refused to accept an Academy Award for his role in "The Godfather."
28	1797	The washing machine was patented in New Hampshire.
29	1973	The last U.S. troops left Vietnam, ending America's military involvement in the Vietnam War.
30	1923	The RMS Laconia arrived in New Work, completing the first voyage around the globe by a passenger ship.
31	1492	King Ferdinand and Queen Isabella of Spain ordered all Jews to be expelled from Spanish soil unless they were willing to convert to Christianity.

April

monday	tuesday	wednesday	thursday
	1 April Fool's Day	2	3
7	8	9	10
14	15	16	17
21	22 Earth Day	23	24
28	29	30	

2025

friday	saturday	sunday
4	5	6
11	12	13 Passover
18 Good Friday	19	20 Easter
25	26	27

April

This Month in History

1	1976	Apple Inc. was founded by Steve Jobs, Steve Wozniak, and Ronald Wayne.
2	1800	German composer Ludwig van Beethoven premiered his First Symphony.
3	1973	The first mobile phone call is held in Manhattan.
4	1949	12 nations formed NATO, the North Atlantic Treaty.
5	1984	Kareem Abdul-Jabbar broke the all-time career scoring record in basketball with 31,419 points.
6	1917	The US declared war on Germany, officially entering World War I.
7	1948	The World Health Organization was established by the UN with the mission of fighting worldwide diseases and epidemics.
8	1904	New York City officially changed the name of Longacre Square to Times Square, in honor of the New Your Times' offices.
9	2005	Prince Charles of England married his second wife, Camilla Parker Bowles.
10	1970	Paul McCartney left the Beatles, effectively breaking up the band.
11	2006	Iran announced that it had managed to enrich uranium.
12	1861	The American Civil War began with an attack on Fort Sumter.
13	1970	The Apollo 13 crew famously communicated, "Houston, we've had a problem" after a oxygen tank explosion.
14	1865	U.S. President Abraham Lincoln was shot by assassin John Wilkes Booth.

15	1912	The RMS Titanic sank slowly into the Atlantic ocean.
16	1964	The Rolling Stones released their debut album, "The Rolling Stones."
17	2011	"Game of Thrones" premiered on HBO.
18	1949	Ireland became an independent republic.
19	1897	The first Boston Marathon was held and won by John J. McDermott.
20	1902	Marie and Pierre Curie discovered the element radium, later winning a Nobel Prize for their discovery.
21	1509	Henry VIII was crowned King of England.
22	1876	Composer Pyotr Ilyich Tchaikovsky completed his ballet, "Swan Lake".
23	1985	Coca-Cola introduced "New Coke," which would turn out to be wildly unpopular.
24	1184 BC	The Greeks secretly entered Troy in the Trojan Horse.
25	1953	The double helix structure of the DNA was explained in a publication by Francis Crick and James D. Watson.
26	1514	Copernicus made his first observation of Saturn.
27	1840	The foundation stone was laid for the Palace of Westminster in London.
28	1916	Ferruccio Lamborghini, the founder of the Lamborghini auto company, was born.
29	1661	The Chinese Ming dynasty occupied Taiwan.
30	1945	Adolf Hitler committed suicide with his one-day wife Eva in a bunker in Berlin.

May

Military Appreciation Month

monday	tuesday	wednesday	thursday
			1
5 Cinco de Mayo	6	7	8
12	13	14	15
19	20	21	22
26 Memorial Day	27	28	29

2025

friday	saturday	sunday
2	3	4
9	10	11 Mother's Day
16	17 Armed Forces Day	18
23	24	25
30	31	

May

This Month in History

1	1950	Gwendolyn Brooks became the first African American to win the Pulitzer Prize for her poetry book, "Annie Allen".
2	2008	"Iron Man", the first movie in the Marvel Cinematic Universe, was released starring Robert Downey Jr.
3	1979	Margaret Thatcher was elected the first female British Prime Minister.
4	1959	The first Grammy Awards were presented, with winners including Frank Sinatra and Ella Fitzgerald.
5	2000	The Sun, Earth, Mercury, Venus, Mars, Jupiter and Saturn all aligned, leading to morbid "Doomsday" predictions.
6	1994	Queen Elizabeth II opened the Channel Tunnel, linking the UK with mainland Europe.
7	1945	Germany's Nazi regime surrendered unconditionally, effectively ending World War II in Europe.
8	1886	Coca-Cola was (supposedly) invented by Dr. John Styth Pemberton in Atlanta, while trying to patent a medicine.
9	1949	American singer Billy Joel was born.
10	1994	Nelson Mandela was sworn in as South Africa's first black president.
11	1958	Minnesota was admitted as the 32nd U.S. state.
12	1941	The world's first fully automatic computer, the Z3, was presented to the world.
13	1950	The first Formula One World Championship season opened.
14	1973	The U.S. space station Skylab was launched.

15	1930	*Ellen Church became the first airline stewardess.*
16	1975	*Junko Tabei of Japan became the first woman ever to reach Mount Everest's summit.*
17	1990	*The World Health Organization removed homosexuality from its list of mental diseases.*
18	1917	*The U.S. Congress passed the Selective Service act and began calling up civilians to fight in World War I.*
19	1962	*Marilyn Monroe gave her last performance, singing Happy Birthday to President John F. Kennedy.*
20	1873	*Blue jeans were patented by Levi Strauss and Jacob Davis.*
21	1904	*FIFA, the Fédération Internationale de Football Association, was founded.*
22	1906	*The Wright brothers patented their "flying machine."*
23	1785	*Benjamin Franklin announced his invention of the bifocals.*
24	1956	*The first Eurovision Song Contest was held and won by Lys Assia of Switzerland.*
25	585	*Thales of Greece made the first recorded prediction of a solar eclipse.*
26	1896	*Nicholas II, the last Russian czar, is crowned.*
27	1851	*The world's first chess tournament was held in London.*
28	1937	*The German automobile manufacturer Volkswagen was founded.*
29	1848	*Wisconsin became the thirtieth U.S. state.*
30	1889	*The brassiere was invented.*
31	1930	*Actor, director, and politician Clint Eastwood was born.*

June   *Pride Month*

monday	tuesday	wednesday	thursday
2 Shavuot	3	4	5
9	10	11	12
16	17	18	19
23 / 30	24	25	26

2025

friday	saturday	sunday
		1
6	7	8
	Eid al-Adha	Pentecost
13	14	15
	Flag Day	Father's Day
20	21	22
27	28	29
Muharram		

June

This Month in History

1	452	Italy was invaded by Attila the Hun.
2	1953	Queen Elizabeth II was crowned in a festive coronation in Westminster Abbey.
3	1492	The first globe of the Earth was unveiled by German geographer Martin Behaim.
4	1783	The Montgolfier brothers demonstrate the first hot air balloon.
5	1981	The Centers for Disease Control and Prevention reported the first cases of AIDS.
6	1930	Frozen food was first sold in retail stores.
7	1968	The world's first Legoland resort opened in Billund, Denmark.
8	793	Vikings raided the Northumbrian coast of England.
9	1986	NASA published their report on the Challenger space shuttle disaster.
10	1926	Famed Spanish architect Antoni Gaudí died.
11	2002	"American Idol" premiered for its first season on Fox.
12	1967	The Supreme Court ruled that states could not ban interracial marriages.
13	1920	The U.S. Post Office Department ruled that children may not be sent to their grandparents by post.
14	1775	The U.S. Army was officially founded.
15	1667	The first human blood transfusion was administered when blood was successfully transfused from a sheep into a 15-year-old.

16	1910	The first Father's Day was celebrated in Washington.
17	1885	The Statue of Liberty arrived in New York after journeying from France.
18	1942	Beatles singer Paul McCartney was born.
19	1978	The first Garfield comic strip appeared in 41 newspapers.
20	1837	Victoria is crowned Queen of England at age 18.
21	1970	In the FIFA World Cup final, Brazil and Pelé become first team and player to win the title three times.
22	1633	The Catholic Church forced scientist Galileo Galilei to renounce his heliocentric world view and state that the Earth is the center of the universe.
23	1894	The International Olympic Committee (IOC) was founded.
24	1901	18-year-old artist Pablo Picasso opened his first art exhibition in Paris.
25	1950	The Korean War began.
26	1924	American troops left the Dominican Republic after eight years of occupation.
27	1927	The U.S. Marines adopted the English bulldog as their mascot.
28	1911	Samuel J. Battle became the first African-American policeman in New York City.
29	1613	Shakespeare's Globe Theatre in London burned down during a performance of "Henry VIII".
30	1971	The crew of three aboard the Soviet spacecraft "Soyuz 11" tragically died after the loss of air supply due to a faulty valve.

July

monday	tuesday	wednesday	thursday
	1	2	3
7	8	9	10
14 Bastille Day	15	16	17
21	22	23	24
28	29	30	31

2025

friday	saturday	sunday
4	5	6
11	12	13
18	19	20
25	26	27 Parents' Day

July

This Month in History

1	1903	The first Tour de France began.
2	1937	Aviator Amelia Earhart disappeared over the Pacific Ocean while attempting to make the first round-the-world flight along the equator.
3	1944	Soviet forces recaptured Minsk from the Germans.
4	1912	The 48-star American flag, with its addition of New Mexico as a state, was adopted.
5	1811	Venezuela became the first South American country to declare independence from Spain.
6	1957	Althea Gibson became the first Black tennis player to win a Wimbledon singles title when she defeated Darlene Hard.
7	1898	The United States annexed Hawaii.
8	1947	A weather balloon crashed in a ranch near Roswell Army Air Field and caused many to belive a flying saucer had been recovered.
9	1937	A fire at 20th Century Fox's facility in New Jersey destroyed most of the studio's silent films.
10	1940	The Battle of Britain began when the Luftwaffe started attacking southern England.
11	1859	The huge bell insinde London's Big Ben tower chimed for the first time.
12	1543	England's King Henry VIII married his sixth and final wife, Catherine Parr.
13	2011	California became the first state to add lessons about LGBTQ to social studies classes in public schools.
14	1789	The French Revolution started when citizens stormed the Bastille prison in Paris.
15	1916	The Boeing company was founded in Seattle.

16	1951	The novel "The Catcher in the Rye" by J.D. Salinger was first published by Little, Brown and Co.
17	1936	The Spanish Civil War began.
18	1918	South African President Nelson Mandela was born in Mvezo.
19	1990	Baseball's all-time hits leader, Pete Rose, was sentenced in Cincinnati to five months in prison for tax evasion.
20	1944	An attempted assassination of Adolf Hitler failed when a bomb exploded but did not injure him.
21	2011	The Atlantis shuttle completed its 135th mission and landed safely in Florida for the last time.
22	1942	Nazis began transporting Jews from the Warsaw Ghetto to the Treblinka concentration camp.
23	2011	Singer Amy Winehouse died in her home at age 27 from alcohol poisoning.
24	1969	The Apollo 11 crew landed safely in the Pacific Ocean after their successful moon mission.
25	1978	Louise Joy Brown, the first baby to be conceived through IVF, was born.
26	2016	Hillary Clinton became the first woman to be nominated for president in the U.S.
27	1953	The Korean War ended after three years of fighting.
28	1976	An earthquake in northern China killed at least 242,000 people.
29	1981	Prince Charles married Lady Diana Spencer at St. Paul's Cathedral in London.
30	1956	"In God We Trust" replaced the national American motto, instead of "E Pluribus Unum" (one out of many).
31	1970	"The Huntley-Brinkley Report" was renamed "NBC Nightly News."

August

monday	tuesday	wednesday	thursday
4	5	6	7
11	12	13	14
18	19	20	21
25	26	27	28

2025

friday	saturday	sunday	
1	2	3	. . . .
8	9	10	. . . .
15	16	17	. . . .
22	23	24	. . . .
29	30	31	. . . .

August

This Month in History

1	2013	Russia granted the NSA mole Edward Snowden temporary asylum in Moscow.
2	1939	Albert Einstein wrote a letter to President Roosevelt expressing his support of an atomic weapons research program.
3	1981	U.S. air traffic controllers went on strike and were consequently fired.
4	1916	The U.S. signed an agreement to purchase the Danish Virgin Islands for $25 million.
5	1962	Marilyn Monroe was found dead in her home in Los Angeles.
6	1945	The first nuclear bomb was exploded in Hiroshima, resulting in 140,000 deaths.
7	2017	Medical examiners said the remains of a man who'd been killed at the World Trade Center on 9/11 had been identified, nearly 16 years after the attacks.
8	1974	President Nixon announced his resignation following the controversial Watergate scandal.
9	2016	Michael Phelps earned the 20th and 21st Olympic gold medals of his career in the 200-meter butterfly and 4x200 freestyle relay.
10	1821	Missouri became the 24th state.
11	2014	Academy Award-winning actor and comedian Robin Williams died by suicide.
12	1981	IBM introduced its first personal computer, model 5150.
13	1961	Germany sealed the border between Eastern and Western Berlin and began building the Berlin Wall.
14	1997	Timothy McVeigh was sentenced to death by lethal injection for the Oklahoma City bombing.

15	1769	Napoleon Bonaparte was born in Corsica.
16	2020	California's Death Valley recorded a temperature of 130 degrees, the third-highest temperature ever measured.
17	1945	"Animal Farm" by George Orwell was published in London.
18	1963	James Meredith became the first Black student to graduate from the University of Mississippi.
19	1848	The New York Herald first reported the discovery of gold in California.
20	1955	Hundreds of people were killed in anti-French rioting in Morocco and Algeria.
21	2010	Fuel was loaded into Iran's first nuclear power plant.
22	1914	Austria-Hungary declared war against Belgium.
23	1914	Japan declared war on Germany in World War I.
24	2006	Pluto was demoted to the status of "dwarf planet" by the International Astronomical Union.
25	1609	Galileo demonstrated his first telescope to lawmakers in Venice.
26	55 B.C.	Julius Caesar and his forces attempted unsuccessfully to invade Britain.
27	1883	The Krakatoa volcano erupted in Indonesia, claiming 36,000 lives.
28	1963	Martin Luther King gave his famous "I have a dream" speech in Washington D.C.
29	1966	The Beatles performed their last public concert in San Francisco.
30	1993	"The Late Show with David Letterman" premiered.
31	1997	Princess Diana died tragically in a car accident in Paris.

September

monday	tuesday	wednesday	thursday
1 Labor Day	2	3	4
8	9	10	11 Patriot Day
15	16 Stepfamily Day	17 Citizenship Day	18
22	23 Rosh Hashana	24	25
29	30		

2025

friday	saturday	sunday
5	6	7 Grandparents' Day
12	13	14
19	20	21
26	27	28

September

This Month in History

1	1985	The wreckage of the Titanic was located on the ocean floor after 73 years.
2	1945	Japan officially surrendered, ending World War II.
3	1943	Allied forces invaded Italy during World War II.
4	1781	Los Angeles was founded by Spanish settlers.
5	1961	President John F. Kennedy signed legislation declaring aircraft hijackings a federal crime.
6	2007	International opera singer Luciano Pavarotti died in Italy at the age of 71.
7	1968	A feminist protest was held outside the Miss America pageant in New Jersey.
8	2022	Queen Elizabeth II died at age 96 after reigning for more than 70 years.
9	1948	The People's Democratic Republic of Korea was declared.
10	2016	John Hinkley Jr., President Ronald Reagan's attempted assissin, was released from St. Elizabeth Psychiatric Hospital.
11	1997	Scotland voted to form its own Parliament following 290 years of union with England.
12	1959	The Soviet Union launched the Luna 2 space probe, which later crash-landed on the moon.
13	2010	Rafael Nadal won his first U.S. Open title after defeating Novak Djokovic.
14	2020	Astronomers reported possible sign of life on Venus, after detecting phosphine in the planet's atmosphere.
15	1821	Costa Rica, El Salvador, Guatemala, Honduras, and Nicaragua declared independence from the Spanish Empire.

16	1848	France abolished slavery in all its territories.
17	1862	The Battle of Antietam led to the bloodiest day of the Civil War, with at least 4,000 dead.
18	1947	The CIA officially came into existence.
19	1934	Bruno Hauptmann was arrested for the Lindbergh baby kidnapping.
20	2019	Greta Thunberg led the world's biggest protest on climate change with students from 185 countries.
21	1947	Author Stephen King was born in Portland, Maine.
22	1994	The "Friends" sitcom premiered on NBC.
23	1932	The kingdoms of Nejd and Hejaz merged to form the Kingdom of Saudi Arabia.
24	1894	F. Scott Fitzgerald, known for writing "The Great Gatsby", was born.
25	1983	38 IRA prisoners escaped Maze Prison in Northern Ireland, in the largest prison breakout in British history.
26	1687	The Acropolis in Athens was attacked by the Venetian army, causing permanent damage to the Parthenon.
27	1905	Einstein's $E=mc^2$ equation was first introduced by physics journal Annalen der Physik.
28	2008	Falcon 1, the first privately supported and funded spacecraft, was launched into space on its fourth attempt by SpaceX.
29	1793	Tennis was mentioned for the first time ever in a British sporting magazine.
30	1960	The animated series The Flintstones premiered on TV.

October

monday	tuesday	wednesday	thursday
		1	2 Yom Kippur
6	7	8	9 Sukkot
13 Columbus Day	14	15	16
20	21	22	23
27	28	29	30

_2025_

friday	saturday	sunday
3	4	5
10	11	12
17	18	19
24	25	26
31 Halloween		

October

This Month in History

1	1867	Karl Marx published "Das Kapital", his description of the capitalist system.
2	1909	Orville Wright broke the altitude record, flying at 1,600 feet.
3	1990	East and West Germany were united as one nation after 40 years of division.
4	1965	Pope Paul VI arrived in New York to become the first Pope to visit the Western hemisphere.
5	1962	James Bond made his theatrical debut in Mr. No, played by Sean Connery.
6	1995	Swiss scientists announced the first discovery of an exoplanet orbiting a sun-like star.
7	1959	The Soviet Luna 3 spacecraft sent back the first ever photographed pictures of the dark side of the moon.
8	1921	The first live radio football game was broadcast over radio from the University of Pittsburgh.
9	1949	Harvard Law School admitted its first female students.
10	1964	Yoshinori Sakai, who was born in Hiroshima on the day the atomic bomb was dropped, lit the Olympic flame during the opening ceremony in the first Olympics to be held in Asia.
11	2000	NASA celebrated launching its 100th Space Shuttle mission.
12	1979	Douglas Adam's "The Hitchhiker's Guide to the Galaxy" was first sold in bookstores.
13	1792	Construction of the White House began, under the direction of Irish architect James Hoban.
14	1926	Winnie the Pooh made his literary debut.

15	2003	China launched its first manned space mission, Shenzhou I.
16	1923	The Walt Disney company was founded by brothers Walt and Roy.
17	1814	A brewery flooded in London, releasing 610,000 liters of beer onto the streets.
18	1867	The territory of Alaska was purchased by the U.S. from Russia for $7.2 million.
19	1954	The 6th highest mountain peak in the world, Cho Oyu, was scaled for the first time.
20	1818	The United States and Britain established the border between Canada and the U.S.
21	1959	The Guggenheim Museum in New York opened its doors to the public.
22	1964	Jean Paul Satre turned down the Nobel Prize for Literature, fearing that it may impact his writing.
23	2001	The first iPod music player was announced by Apple.
24	1926	Escape artist Houdini performed for the last time in Michigan.
25	1955	The first microwave oven was sold.
26	1905	Norway signed a treaty of separation with Sweden.
27	1971	The Democratic Republic of the Congo was renamed Zaire.
28	1955	Bill Gates, chairman and CEO of Microsoft, was born.
29	1863	The Red Cross humanitarian institution was founded.
30	1938	H.G. Wells' "War of the Worlds" was broadcast over radio, leading to a panic over a suspected alien invasion.
31	1941	Mount Rushmore memorial was completed after 14 years of construction.

November

monday	tuesday	wednesday	thursday
3	4	5	6
10	11 Veterans' Day	12	13
17	18	19	20
24	25	26	27 Thanksgiving

2025

friday	saturday	sunday
	1	2 Daylight Saving Ends
7	8	9
14	15	16
21	22	23
28 Black Friday	29	30

November

This Month in History

1	1512	Michelangelo's painting on the Sistine Chapel ceiling is exhibited for the first time.
2	1982	Ronald Reagan established Martin Luther King, Jr. Day.
3	1954	The Japanese science fiction movie "Godzilla" was released.
4	1952	The National Security Agency (NSA) was formed.
5	1943	Vatican City was bombed during World War II.
6	1814	Adolphe Sax, Belgian inventor of the saxophone, was born.
7	1921	Benito Mussolini declared himself the leader of the National Fascist Party in Italy.
8	1895	German physicist Wilhelm Conrad Röntgen accidentally discovered X-rays.
9	1985	Gary Kasparov won the 13th World Chess Championship to become the youngest champion at age 22.
10	1903	The windshield wiper was patented by inventor Mary Anderson.
11	1926	The numbered highway system in the U.S. was approved.
12	1968	The U.S. Supreme Court cancelled an Arkansas law banning the teaching of evolution in public schools.
13	1862	Lewis Carroll began writing "The Adventures of Alice in Wonderland".
14	2010	23-year-old Sebastian Vettel became the youngest person to win the Formula One World Championship.

15	1952	Newark Airport reopened after closing earlier that year due to increased accidents.
16	1945	The United Nations Educational, Scientific and Cultural Organization, UNESCO, was founded.
17	1558	Queen Elizabeth I became the Queen of England.
18	1883	Four official timezones were adopted in North America.
19	1952	The first commercial air route from Canada to Europe was opened by Scandinavian Airlines.
20	1985	Windows 1.0 was released by Microsoft.
21	1941	The cartoon canary bird Tweety made its first TV appearance.
22	1963	American president John F. Kennedy was assassinated by Lee Harvey Oswald in Texas.
23	1976	Jacques Mayol, AKA Dolphin Man, was the first person to dive 100 meters below the surface of the sea without any breathing equipment.
24	1859	Charles Darwin published his groundbreaking book, "On the Origin of Species."
25	1920	The first Thanksgiving parade was held in Philadelphia.
26	1789	America celebrated its first national Thanksgiving holiday.
27	2005	The first successful face transplant was carried out in France on a woman who had been mauled by a dog.
28	1868	Mt. Etna in Sicily erupted violently.
29	1899	FC Barcelona was founded by footballer Hans Gamper.
30	1982	Michael Jackson's second solo album, Thriller, was released.

December

monday	tuesday	wednesday	thursday
1 Cyber Monday	2	3	4
8	9	10	11
15 Hanukkah	16	17	18
22	23	24 Christmas Eve	25 Christmas Day
29	30	31 New Year's Eve	

2025

friday	saturday	sunday
5	6	7 Pearl Harbor Remembrance Day
12	13	14
19	20	21
26	27	28

December

This Month in History

1	1918	The kingdom of Iceland was established as a sovereign state.
2	1804	Napoleon Bonaparte crowned himself Emperor of France in the Notre Dame Cathedral.
3	1818	Illinois joined the Union as the 21st state.
4	1980	The British rock band Led Zeppelin disbanded after 12 years following the death of their drummer.
5	1901	Walt Disney was born.
6	1921	Ireland gained independence from Britian, forming the Irish Free State.
7	1787	Delaware became the first state to accept the U.S. constitution.
8	2010	SpaceX launched, orbited, and recovered its spacecraft, becoming the first private company to do so.
9	1950	Harry Gold was sentenced to 30 years in prison for relaying atomic bomb secrets to the Soviet Union.
10	1901	The very first Nobel Prizes were awarded.
11	2008	Bernie Madoff was arrested for his long-standing Ponzi scheme.
12	1963	Kenya declared its independence from the UK.
13	2003	Saddam Hussein, the President of Iraq, was captured by American forces.
14	1900	Quantum theory was presented at the Physics Society in Berlin.
15	2009	The Boeing 787 Dreamliner took its maiden flight.

16	1707	Mont Fuji in Japan erupted, with the eruption lasting 17 days.
17	1989	The first episode of "The Simpsons" aired.
18	1956	Japan joined the United Nations.
19	1154	Henry II was crowned king of England.
20	1963	A seven-day Christmas accord allowed thousands to cross the Berlin Wall and visit their relatives.
21	1898	Chemists Marie and Pierre Curie discovered the radioactive element radium.
22	1882	The first Christmas tree to be decorated with electric lights was displayed in New York City.
23	1888	Painter Vincent van Gogh cut off his ear in the midst of a psychotic break.
24	1865	The white supremacist extremist group, Ku Klux Klan, was formed.
25	352	The first recorded Christmas was celebrated.
26	1941	The U.S. set Thanksgiving Day as the fourth Thursday in November.
27	1831	Charles Darwin set off on his 5-year journey to study the theory of evolution.
28	1836	South Australia became a colony under British rule.
29	1852	Police in Boston arrested teenager Emma Snodgrass for wearing pants in public.
30	1919	Lincoln's Inn in London admitted its first female bar student.
31	2009	A Blue Moon and solar eclipse occurred on the same day.

www.ingramcontent.com/pod-product-compliance
Lightning Source LLC
LaVergne TN
LVHW020425070526
838199LV00003B/281